KISSES
OF
DEATH

POEMS BY
CHANTELLE SCHENCK

KISSES OF DEATH
POEMS BY CHANTELLE SCHENCK

iUniverse books may be ordered through booksellers or by contacting:

iUniverse
1663 Liberty Drive
Bloomington, IN 47403
www.iuniverse.com
1-800-Authors (1-800-288-4677)

ISBN: 978-1-5320-7684-8 (sc)
ISBN: 978-1-5320-7685-5 (e)

Print information available on the last page.

iUniverse rev. date: 06/27/2019

This book is dedicated to my brothers, Micah and Javone

To my ignorant muses

And to all who have kissed death

. . . Sometimes death leads to life

CONTENTS

INTRODUCTION

I thought long and hard about publishing this book. There is something final in printing your thoughts, your feelings, and your emotions for all to see. You give people a glimpse into your soul.

Most people hide who they really are because of fear. They fear rejection and judgment. I have learned that there is nothing to fear. Life is about progression and connection. It is a progressive journey, and your connections with people effect how you live life.

Every day we find out something new about ourselves. When you are faced with the truth of who you have chosen to be, you have a wonderful opportunity. You can decide to embrace what you have become, or you can be the person God has created you to be.

This is a book of reflection. Some of the poetry is very personal. Some of it is very random. Some of it is inspired by people and events. I've learned that it is okay to feel. It is okay to express what is inside of you. Expression can create connection, and we connect with the fact that we are not alone in our insane emotions. Every obstacle and every victory reveals weakness and strength. The key is being able to live in truth. The truth will set you free and keep you free.

The truth of God's word brings light, illumination, and correction. God is never intimidated by our issues and dysfunctions. He only asks that we turn to him in every instance. This poetry is about emotional affairs and emotional release. I believe that there is such a need for mental and spiritual restoration. Many people are walking around with scarred souls because of past relationships and rejection. More than anything, I want you to be inspired. I want you to be empowered. Never be ashamed of your journey. Be ashamed of not becoming the best version of yourself.

In everything I've learned that no matter how I feel, or what I see, everything must be judged by the word of God. Everything that I am must submit to the Word of God, even the longings of my own will. I am honored that you have taken out the time to read this book. It is my desire that you walk away valuing the restoration of your soul.

LONGING

The following poetry is dedicated to anyone who has ever been sick with longing. There is nothing wrong with longing; there is nothing wrong with natural desire. It is only natural. There is something wrong with allowing these emotions to dictate your thoughts and actions, however. You can long for someone so much that it can begin to control your life. It is easy to get lost in a feeling, and to get caught up in lust and infatuation. People stop living because of hurtful relationships. People pursue toxic relationships because they refuse to take control of their emotions. We all have entered into relationships knowing from that start that it wasn't God's best for us. We want what we want more than we want God's will at times. Loneliness, a lack of self respect, and rebellion keep us entrapped and stagnated. It is so important though that we stay connected with the love of God.

His love allows us to see clearly. The truth is that a person should never be your lifeline; that position belongs to God. It is a warped mentality to think that you can't live without the love and affection of someone who does not genuinely love you. A man or woman may be the object of our affection, but should not be the source of our existence. Your emotional stability can't hinge on a person's response to you. God alone is the lover of your soul and the strength of your life. As you live and love, never forget that God is the mender of the brokenhearted. Let Him be everything that your soul longs for.

CHRONICLES OF A SICK SOUL

These are chronicles of a sick soul
A heart grown cold
Passions and lusts transparently told
A time of great instability
A loss of vision
A relax of control

These are the transgressions of an unrenewed mind
Self-deception, rebellion, and pride
The blueprints of a deadly fortress
A damaged self-portrait
A mission aborted

How swiftly devotion slips away
And we become changed
God
Have Mercy
If not for your Grace
There is Mercy
There is Grace

MERCY

I should be asleep
Peacefully dreaming
But instead
I find myself
Lost in thoughts of you
I'm trying to find my way out
But this maze is very intricate and detailed
And I can't see through this self-imposed haze
I've been running around in circles
For never-ending days
The sun shines on my captured mind
But I shield my eyes
I decide to meditate
And with every thought
My soul becomes deeply rooted
My body becomes stable in desire
My spirit becomes imprisoned
Beating on the doors of my heart
My spirit pleads with me to stop
Before it's too late
But I fear it's already too late
So I am lost
Trying to escape
This unhealthy fate
This premeditated destination
I can't help myself
Maybe I can
But I just chose
Not to
God have mercy on me
Have mercy on my curiosity

SICK WITH LOVE

I did not know that my heart was so soft and never shaped
I had no clue of how quickly it could be formed
That my passion could be so demanding and blinding
I did not think that I could succumb and become sick with love
I am so extraordinary, and yet I yielded my soul to someone so common
And now he has made me less than common
What I spent a lifetime achieving, he destroyed with just one look
He broke down an empire with the turning of his head
How could he be so dumb?
I am everything and he is in need of me, but right now
He cannot see
But I am fully aware
I know who I am and still my soul clings to him
Longing for his affection
Imagining his touch
Wanting to hear his song
All the while understanding that completion of this affair
Should never be
I am emotionally entangled and I am sick with love
The hour comes and I think of him
The sun rises and I think of him
And I want him to be filled with me
To be moved by me
Yet there is a place inside my heart that is
So powerful and strong
A love that reminds me of my worth
Always speaking of how priceless I am
And when I pause to look into his soul
I know the truth

He is not worthy of me
I love fully, with all my heart, with no conditions
And all that I give when it comes to love
Must be given to me
Because I would live
To love him
But instead
He makes me sick
With love

POLITELY

You invade my thoughts and
Challenge my standard
You make me forget about the
Promise I've made
I look into you and I am tempted
I want you to kiss me, but my lips are
Sealed
I would touch you, but then you would demand
Your fill of love
And if you touched me
I would not have the strength to remove your hand.
Your passion is contagious
And I want to savor it all
I look at you and I am drawn into fire
I think that it's your eyes — how beautiful and
Telling they are
Eyes that contain compassion
And unrestraint
I see the unbridled lust that lay just
Beneath the window to your soul
I can tell you are wild, although
You are a master at being reserved
Simmering underneath is uncontrolled
Decadence and if you unleashed your
Desire you could not stop, and you would not stop
Because you are a slave to pleasure
If you would pleasure me, I would be enslaved to you.
And all sanity would be lost
And so I will not close my eyes and receive your

Kiss upon my lips. And I will fold my
Hands politely on my lap. I will become immune
To your smile and arousing
Intellect
And you will never know the depth of
My desire
I would rather let it burn and be apart
Then burn with you in hell.

COLD

Some things are better left unsaid
But I believe that everything should be said
Although it has broken my heart
And the hurt still sits on me
Heavy
Like lead
I desire him
He desires others
The pain is intense
Oh, help me father
I'm so tired
Tired of being left for dead
For giving my soul
I am growing cold of giving my soul
But there is nothing left to do
Only to except the truth
I asked for truth
I can't help but clearly see that
He never really wanted me
He never really cared for me
He just treaded very lightly
Never cared to see into me
I see traces of psychology
My heart is feeling like stone
And I don't want to be
Cold
I am growing cold
Growing cold from
Giving my soul
I'm so tired of being left for dead
My soul feels dead

FROM HIS KISS

I am irritated with desire for you
Frustrated with how quickly my thoughts
Turn to you
Appalled by how my body is yearning
For you
You are consuming me and I don't know
What to do
I am torn between my heart and my lust
I know that you would never give me enough
And I know that you don't deserve my love
Nothing about you warrants my touch
I can't seem to let you know and must
Not want to let it go, but I am losing all
Control, still I can't seem to let it go
So many times I've tried to stay away
You make it easy by what you say
And how you do me
I just want you out of my head
I can't stay the fool or I will
End up dead
Sometimes I wonder how you feel
I think you know your appeal
Tell me, Love, what I shall do
I just need to be free of you
Right now, nothing satisfies
But I won't live in compromise
I am so much better than this
But why do I long to feel your kiss?
I know better than this
I am so much better than this
I can't allow you to make me common

Lord, You must reveal the promise
I'm tired and I am through
I need to wash my hands of wanting you
Father, help me in this
Or else I will die from his kiss

ANGRY WITH LUST

I am angry with lust and drunk with desire
I need to get sober for I am playing with fire
My mind is running and creating a place
Where you and I are together
In the wrong kind of ways
I am drifting away from stable shores
I have opened too many doors
And now I ache for you
My mind is sick with you
I need to be released from you
I am tired of being in need of you
But maybe those are just words
Just the right things to say
And maybe I just want to ease my conscious
If only for a moment and then I
Will get back to normal
I've never been this far gone
Never felt so strong for so long
I can't release my grip for
Holding on. My heart is assuring
Me that wanting you is no good for me
Why do I chase the forbidden thing?
Knowing that you're no good for me
I fear that if I cross the line
You will not find the life I find
I can't keep indulging in you
Or I will do the things that I
Should not do. I will say the thing
That I should not say
And the primal part of me will be displayed
But I must consider and I must judge

Do you even value me?
Do you even clearly see?
I think that you just lead me on
I think you delight in
Claiming my thoughts
Why do I feel so wild? You don't even love me now.

IF ONLY FOR A MOMENT

For a moment, only for a moment
I will meditate, contemplate
The cycle
And why you
You are the same man that I loved before
But you are all together separate
I wonder at myself and how
I manage
Without being stripped
And placed into mental
Solitude
I know it is wrong but I
Want to use you
To go against my better judgment
And function in the place of
Desire
It is so beneath me
It is sure to enslave me
But if I do not surrender
It will torment me
And for temporary freedom
I would be chained

GIVE TO ME

Will you give me what I am asking of you?
Will you forget about consequence?
Will you let it all play out?
Sequence by sequence?
Let it play out
Then repent
I already need forgiveness
I want to touch you so badly
Let it play out
Then repent
Frequently the feeling hits me
I am consistently compelled
And so I have to catch myself
I constantly censor how I feel
I don't know if it's wrong
I just know that the feelings are strong
At times they drown me out
They bury all common sense
And before I know it I am reaching for you
Even when your embrace takes the life out of me
I want to shower you with kisses in all types of places
Let your passion keep me sedated
Intoxicated, I am drunk with your love
I will give you whatever you want
Speak your heart
I will come
Will you let it play out?
Sequence by sequence?
Let it play out
Then repent.

ODE TO THE IRISHMAN

It's not fair that you came to my mind while I was alone with my thoughts
Late in the evening with no sounds distracting me
And with no one and nothing to create the boundary that separates
You from me and me from my heart

By now I should be free of you
But it seems that in the moments of truth
When I am in need of a gentle touch
Or a serenade of words

I find my soul still calls for you
Although I know on the surface
You don't belong to me
Nor do I belong to you

My eyes seek you out
Searching through my memories
So that I can replay our encounters again
It doesn't even matter
That while I long for you
You don't even recall me

What have you done?
What type of spell have you put on my heart?
To make me love you in a timeless manner

What have you whispered in my ear?
To alter my hearing
You have made me dumb
To the point that I don't have
To hear you say
I Love You
The actions of a fool

This cycle of desire stagnates
There is no need to impose
Torture on my hungry heart

Just give me you
And I will give you me
It is the only answer that I have
It may stop this insane addiction

For I cannot form the words or get the strength to speak on my passion
for you
So for now I will think of you, dream of you
And maybe tomorrow I will find the courage to tell you

The depth of my love.

TO WHOM IT MAY CONCERN

It is 2 a.m. in the morning and I should be asleep. I am angry with myself because it is happening again. All the signs are there, and I know myself. I'm really not sure if it is right or wrong to long for someone the way that I long for you. I don't even really know who you are. I just know the surface things, and then my own personal judgment of your character. From what I do know, I am sure that I want to love you. I am 100% positive that your life would be better with my love.

I am so frustrated with myself. I seem to always let my heart be drawn out like a magnet. My heart blossoms without sunshine or water. It seems to be so fertile that it is scary. I don't think that it is natural to feel the way that I feel about you. This is too intense, and too strong. All I know is that I need for the cycles to end. My heart has to stop this. It has to stop this. I am going crazy inside. Help me. I feel trapped. I feel doomed. I feel that this road will lead to the worst kind of heartache. I should walk way and be clean and unscarred.

I need to go to sleep. I need direction and peace. If I reveal my heart, I forfeit the power to protect myself from rejection. I think it is simple chemistry. You keep calling me to you, and I really would like to come. But if you turn from me once I get there, I am telling you right now, I am done.

I really don't know, but I feel that is too much power for you to hold. It is like you are the captain of my soul, turning me every which way that you want. I am only human. You are only human, but the way you make me feel is not human at all. This current between you and I is strong enough to drown in. The emotions that you bring out of me are more countless than the sands on every ocean. That is what you do to me, and you will not stop. You have already made your mark on my entire being, you cause the bleeding and you stop the bleeding.

I could be overreacting. I am caught up. I am caught up in the idea of your smile, and the tenderness of your touch. I could be captivated by your words and how beautiful you make me feel. But I don't want to live in a dream. I need to see the reality and if it is dysfunctional I must learn to set me free. I am resting, I am making my heart slow down. I can't keep rushing into love just because of how fast it pounds. My soul is fertile ground.

INSANITY

I've heard that there is a thin line between love and insanity. The average person has temporary moments of insanity. We have all looked back on a situation and wondered, "What was I thinking?" We have all played the fool. We have all been abusive and abused. We look back and see the crazy thought process. Sometimes it is hard to see the obvious when you are head-deep into a situation or relationship. This poetry is about how we choose to think — that gray place we have all lived in before. This poetry speaks about those places of inner turmoil, the insane thoughts that you have when your heart loves someone. It is about the reaching for truth in the midst of all the insanity.

Understand that God is not intimidated by your dysfunction. There is no dysfunction greater than the love and forgiveness of God. You are not alone, all of us have been companions of dysfunction in one way or another at some point in life. When you are disappointed in yourself, don't ever stop reaching for God. When you reach for him, He will always reach back with unconditional love.

THE PERFECT WRONG

Tonight I was human
Tonight I was flawed
Tonight I committed
The Perfect Wrong

The way that you were
I will never forget it
Things happened so fast
In a matter of seconds

You appeared out of nowhere, and set your eyes on me
It was almost like a dream, something out of a movie scene

How did you know to search me out? How was I, so easily found?

Depending on the moment, depending on the setting
I realize now, almost anything can happen

I should've walked away, but I entertained you for too long
Drawn in by your words, they were dirty. They were Raw.
The ultimate temptation for someone Clean…
Was it curiosity, or you that undressed me?

You made your intentions crystal clear
How you leaned in, how your breath grazed my ear
At any other time I would've said no
But I let things slide, 'cause I wanted to know

I can't even believe what I secretly let you do
Behind closed doors, locked in a bathroom

You appeared out of nowhere, and set your eyes on me
Was it a dream? Was it even me?

I can't even recall my mental state
To be seduced in the light
Inside an elevator

You appeared out of nowhere, and set your eyes on me
I played a part in these lustful scenes

This rare occasion

It is all my shame to bear
I was present
Living in the moment
I was conscious
Fully aware

Tonight I was human. Tonight I was flawed.
And tonight I committed
The Perfect Wrong

CONSIDER

You don't even consider my heart
And I do not know why
When so much of what I do
Has been to give you life
You don't consider my heart
And I cannot understand
When I love with no conditions, when you act
Less than a man
You don't consider my heart
And it is oh so cruel
I long to see your passion
But you're calm, collected and cool
If you considered my heart
You would fall to your knees
I should consider my heart
All things considered

ABOUT YOUR GIRL

I'm sure that she is beautiful
I'm sure she is what you need
Please don't take this in the wrong way
But she has nothing to do
With you and me
I've tried to have some empathy
Still. We need to make plans
I am my own woman
And you are your own man
I don't want you forever
Just maybe for a few days and nights
It has absolutely nothing to do with
Wrong
It has everything to do with what feels right
I'm sure that she is intelligent
I'm sure that she challenges your thoughts
But if we were together
It doesn't mean that you and her are not
Look into my eyes
See into my heart
Let me love you
In precious moments
From finish
To start
Let me take you to a place
That you've never been before
I will leave you
Satisfied
And begging
For more
I'm sure she is wonderful

At most times
She is what you need
And technically you are free, you haven't given her a ring
She has no say, let me have my way
She has nothing to do
With you and me
It's not about your girl

CRIMINAL

I love you so much

But I don't want to be a witness

We both know that you are with a criminal

She has broken all the laws of love
And made you to look pathetic, weak and dumb
Now your reflection is disfigured
And you can't see who you really are

She is a criminal

She has committed slander
She has severed you with hateful words
She is a fraud
To even say that she loves you is purgery and very disturbing

She will turn you into a monster, and then flaunt it
I see how you suffer and how you have been diminished
Her crimes are endless, with no repentance

My loyalty is with you
Walk away
Make a clean break

Escape

Or you will become a criminal too
It is your life.
It is your heart.

But I don't want to be a witness to these crimes of "love"

We both know that you are with a criminal

THIS FEELING

I am here again. I am sick
With the fact. I close my eyes, shake my head and then I sigh
Then I write, as tears fill up and then overflow
Because only I know the bruises on my
Tampered heart
Things cannot go on this way, or else
All that I am will die
I feel I am slowly perishing because of all that
I let you do to me
You sit too heavily on my heart
And then you break it into pieces
I can't clearly think because of my own issues
I am tired of how you don't care
I feel as if I've given everything
The most precious parts
I just want your touch, your smile, your affection, your attention
For you to fully listen
I don't like this feeling
This weight on my soul
The struggle to pursue
Or let go
I have been silent for too long
And I must speak
But your eyes silence me. Every single time
I don't speak my mind
And never my heart
I don't like
This Feeling

THE DISCONNECT

There needs to be a disconnect, 'cause
I can't connect with myself
I don't really like the way you make
Me feel about myself
I just don't understand the type of man you are
I seem to lose ground when I look past
Who you are and into your heart
I give you too much credit. It has everything to do with how I see
I need to make a choice about who I am going to be
Without your words, without your touch, I am more than enough
But still I am after your heart, and I would also
Take your soul. It has been my desire for so long
Even when I know you aren't good for me, this is insanity
Part of me wants you
Part of me wants all of the control
Part of me wants to use every ounce of power to bring you near
To speak forbidden words and to do forbidden things
But I am trapped inside my
Innocence
Chained to my own intelligence and
Bound to self-respect
And stagnated by circumstance
I have stayed in control while letting my mind roam
But I am becoming restless
And so I might become bold
I must disconnect because I know the truth
When it comes to how I feel
When it comes to me and you
I need peace and I want a chance to feel
But you won't release me
I must initiate
The Disconnect

CAN'T FUNCTION

I can't function this way
My heart, my mind
I find my soul is unstable
Most of the time.
I get so heavy with you
Just you and nobody else
It is bad for my health
Right now I want to cry
You don't look into my eyes
Babe
Look into my eyes
Do you see how I'm dying?
Slowly
In every moment, with every encounter
The unspoken words are torture
And I feel buried alive
My emotions change
Two days ago I said that I wouldn't care
But then I drowned in your glance
My tongue clung to the roof of my mouth
And I sat silent for hours
What have I allowed you to do to me?
I feel so solid and I become free when I am away
From you
But when I am with you
I lose myself
I'm not myself
I become different
My thoughts are different and there is a shifting
I somehow hear you reaching for me
It is the oddest thing

Lord, I ask for mercy and help
But you keep beckoning me
Begging me to come . . . or is that just what I want?
Is it just vain imagination?
A consuming fantasy?
You and me
This was meant to be
For other reasons
Not for what I'm feeling
I should just tell you once
Kiss you twice
And hold you
If only to get you out of my system
Get Out of My System
I will no longer reason with what
I'm feeling for you
Feelings are feelings
Get Out of My System

DEFILED

I feel that I have defiled
The sacred thing
Giving you so much of me
My words, my thoughts, my strength, my time
I've been entertaining lies
I feel that I have been put to shame
Evaluating all my ways trying to get so much
From you, wanting to be a part of you
I feel that I have lost myself, acting
Out like someone else. Someone with no sense of pride, with every step knowing
Why. With every sentence, with every smile
Having motive all the while. Only wanting
You to see the beauty that lies in me
I feel that you have been cruel
Knowing how much I care for you, allowing
Me to play the fool, humoring me, I've been
Such a fool
I feel that you don't really care
Your world would keep turning
Without me there
You don't sense the gain
You don't recognize the loss
You don't see the treasure
You don't know my cost
I feel that you delight in my want
You like the fact that I am after your heart
You like the fact that I am walking the line
Because I know my desire shines through my eyes
I feel that you don't have a clue
You don't understand my longing for you

Somehow you have attacked my soul
And I am fighting to keep my body
Controlled
I think that I am acting insane
I am oh-so-close to playing the game
Everything is up in the air
I've never been transparent; I wouldn't dare
I feel that I need to face the truth
You look past me
And I look past it
But no more. My heart is numb
And my spirit is sore
I will not beg for your kiss
I will not hunger for your touch
I will not try to ease your heart
You look past me
Consistently
You're not worthy
You are not worthy
So please do not look at me
And smile
Please do not call my name out loud
Please don't act as if you care
Please use your psychology on someone else
Please don't lie, just speak the truth
I'll live
I will not die
Without your love

GONE AWAY

How can you be gone away from me
Distant like the sky and the sea
It is the timeless of tragedies
And still I cannot breathe

The earth shakes beneath my feet and a horrid
Wind blows hitting me hard and violently
My gaze has been silenced and now everything is dark
Silent. Still. Solitude. I am non-responsive. I have no mood
And it is because you have gone away

It was swift. It was quick. It was day and now it is night.
I just spoke your name I just memorized your face. I just envisioned your
beautiful eyes and sighed at the thought of your smile and gentle touch
That was just yesterday
Today
You have gone away

I must find you
So that I can come back to my senses
I must find you
If I am to go on

I must find you because you have gone away from me
And you are in possession of my heart, the tormentor of my soul

I wonder if you meant to steal it
You know that you did
You are quite brilliant
I had no clue

But now it is clear that
You have acted out my worst fear
All the color has left and I see only shades
Following your departure

In time I will laugh again,
But today I will meditate on how
everything changed

With no remorse
You have gone away

Away from

Me

THE BEAUTIFUL LIE

I am at a wonder on
How I lost my soul
You were cooper
All I saw was gold

I've learned that the truth
Comes out in time

But it's so hard to let go of
Such a BEAUTIFUL LIE

So much of who you are
Fulfilled so much of my need
But what meant the most
Was void empty

The place inside your heart
For God alone
Was torn, beaten, deceived
And cold

I know that warmth flowed
From my hand
I have
The faith of a child
You had
The doubt of a man

But there was something in your speech
That captivated my mind

Love,
You are such a BEAUTIFUL LIE

The anguish
The torment
I have been bruised
There was too much pain
In wanting you

How did you get in?
Where was my shield
Because even in your deception
I longed for you
Still

I was caught up
I didn't catch the clues

I was too engrossed
In the thought of you

Your face
Your lips
Your touch
Your eyes
It's so hard to let go
Of such a BEAUTIFUL LIE

Every single night ends the same

I ask for mercy

I speak your name

I know the truth
And at times I slide

It's so hard to say goodbye
To such a BEAUTIFUL LIE

But it is time to say goodbye
MY BEAUTIFUL LIE

THE FALSEHOOD

Forgive me
I didn't know how deceived I was in my thoughts toward you
I don't know why it has taken so long for me to accept the truth
I am really shaken by the things that I find
The intensity of my thoughts, and the path of my mind
I have been in denial for way too long
Trying to understand what is right, and why what I've been feeling is wrong
Trying to keep these feelings and emotions at bay
Trying to keep the innocence between you and me
But I have already wronged you; what should I do?
I have looked at you and lusted
I have talked with you and lusted
I have angered you and lusted
I've had no empathy
Even when you have pleaded with me
I'm not sure when it happened
I can't recall the moment
I have no idea when my heart latched onto you
My heart did this without your permission
Forgive Me
I know that you love another
I know that there is history and I know that there are memories
But you know me
Absolutely no empathy
Does that make me evil?
I hope not
Because I wonder at my destination
Tell me, what am I to do with all this?
What should I do with all that is inside of me?
I think that I should give it to you

But my thoughts are unstable these days
Where do I end up?
Forgive Me
I have kept silent, but silence hasn't set me free
I must tell you what I want from you
You act like you don't already know
I want you to teach me then let me go
I want to be deep in your heart;
I am asking for very much, but I am so much
I can't look in your eyes and lie
I already know the truth
And you are perceptive, too
These are the Falsehoods

WASTE AWAY

I waste away
I waste away in your arms
I deteriorate in your embrace
Brainwashed
By your words
And put to death in your kiss

I waste away
With every second spent
Entertaining you
Clinging to you, instead of truth

Dying with you
Being an accessory to your
Slow suicide
Just as you accommodate mine

You are breaking my will
Redefining my life. Nothing about this is right
It mostly just feels right in the moment
But feelings are fading
They change with the wind

My feelings lie to me
They scream obscenities
The most ruthless part grows
While the beauty ceases
And I waste away
Unchanged, Uninspired
Satisfying the lower nature

Resurrecting what has been put to death
Lord, search me
Purge me
Empower me with Your touch
Bring illumination
So that I can arise from this desolate,
Wasteful place

LIFE

The very nature of life causes us to ask so many questions, but I've learned that life is a series of choices. The beauty of life is in the power of choice. We can choose life, or we can choose death.

The following poetry reflects the different stages of life. It speaks of my thoughts and feelings in reaction to certain instances. It is not all a bed of roses. It is filled with questions, observations, and truths. Life is to be lived. We can go through the motions of just existing, or we can create a beautiful journey. We can see the beauty and wonders that a new day holds. It is an opportunity to do, and to be different from yesterday.

Live with purpose and on purpose. Have faith and maintain it. Don't allow circumstance to dictate your life. Take control. If you do not take control of your life, others will do it for you.

BEFORE

You left me alone
In the cold
In the dark

But not that long ago you swore your allegiance to me
You said it was for a lifetime, and so I let you be my lifeline

My resting place
My security

That was foolish
So now you are cut off
I wrongly thought we were from the same cloth

Now you are cut off

This is a reminder to you and me
I was living Before
Before you

Before you made me catch my breath
I was alive and not at war with myself

My life. My Joy. It is not connected with yours
I was living. I was free. I was productive
Before

You seem to think that you constructed me.
You fulfilled some needs
But you were never the essence of my being

If anything,
your mediocrity slowed things down
It brought me low. It drowned me out.

My vibrancy, my laughter, is not connected with yours
My life. My Joy. Is not connected with yours
I was living. I was free.
Before You, There was Me.

BITTER

I don't want to be bitter when
Looking back on my days
The night quickly comes and the sun sets so swiftly
The time merges together, and when I pause
I find the tragic truth that while I attempt to live, I am leaving life behind
I don't want to regret the ways that I walked my path.
Paying no particular attention
Never soaking in my surroundings
Refusing to stop long enough to ponder the
Road ahead of me
Why should I live
If I can't live free?
I don't want to wait until the beauty of my youth fades
Before I realize that I must create memories, and decide my destiny
I see that where I am is where I have chosen to be
The entire world moves on as I move in my own world
The world I have created for myself
The secret places inside me are beginning to surface
The parts of me that are on display scream for change
And I have ignored my own warnings from my own heart
I have ignored my own warnings from my own heart
If I continue on with my hands over my ears
I know exactly what my future holds
So, to hold on with such a tight grip is a sign
A sign of fear or stupidity
Neither suits me
The lighting strikes. The thunder roars.
Telling me I am made for more
Everything around me vocalizes the truth
In these matters. The truth of the matter.
Life is priceless. My life is a treasure.
Life is a rare gift that was made to be given
Anything less than that is shameful

If I decide to never take control
I am pitiful
If those who love me ignore my deadly flaws
They are pitiful
Just in case tomorrow comes
I make a decision to throw yesterday away
Every hour wasted
Every minute of confusion
And every second of unbelief
If tomorrow comes
I will honor it
I will honor God with my day
I will worship God with my nights
I will choose the path that brings forth change
For the betterment of humanity
I will walk the path that accompanies peace
If I can't live in peace
My life is nothing

I LISTEN FOR YOU

I listen for you
But you are nowhere to be found
The tune of your voice is the same
The same treble, the same sound
But you have left and it breaks my heart
Is it so bad?
Is it so bad?
To have lived a life seeking after what is right
Is it so regretful?
That you choose to be numb
Why can't you see that you shine?
You shine so beautiful like the sun
Why don't you know that this average
Display of yourself is still greatness
So, will you really let him
Will you really let them
Steal your life away?
I know there have been disappointments
One-thousand times over
And failure has happened
That doesn't make you less-than
It proves you are human
I LISTEN FOR YOU
I wait to hear, to see you again
Nothing will change in your silence
Nothing will change in your violence?
There is a process and such things
So don't be the villain in the murder scene
Don't walk away from love
Just be still and let him
Love you
Guide you
Show you

CLEAN

I didn't mean to step into the dirt and bathe in the mud
I slipped and fell
Then soaked in it for a while

I didn't want to put on that filthy coat
But I was cold, and it is comfortable
And it was right within my reach
Now every time I get cold
I reach for the same coat and I am cloaked in dung

I rest in the destitute places
I wallow in the swamps
I sleep with the pigs
I know that I am dirty

I promised myself that I would shower
And be refreshed in the rain
But I don't want to feel the sting
Of cleansing water

It is so much easier to stay buried in mud
But I should be clean

THESE PAGES

These pages are my
Security and freedom
They leave no evidence or proof
And there can be no blood on my hands
Within these pages
I can speak to you. I can say the words
That I should not say
I can tell the truths that I will never tell
And it will remain between you and I
These pages are my will and testament
My hunger and craving for you
My emotions and human intellect
The things at the base of my humanity
The absolute lowest part of my nature
The animalistic creature that would
Disregard common courtesy and morality
Within these pages
There can be no blood on my hands
Can there be?

IN WAITING

I am restless in waiting
I am pointless in my pondering
Thinking on tomorrow and evaluating yesterday
Something is off in my heartbeat
It is not so stable. My soul is chaotic
And moving to places that I don't need
To go

I need something more
Something tangible
Something radiant
Something that sees into my heart
I shine. I am trimmed in gold
Transformation is coming

I wonder at love. I wonder at my loss
Must I conform? Must I become more?
To have more

Excuse my turmoil. But I am nervous
And in shock of this unexpected pain
It feels very familiar. It all is so similar
The outcome that silence brings
The rejection that fear feeds

And I am tired of the strain
Let me be clear
Let me state that my spirit is strong.

Like metal. Like an Oakwood tree. My
Heart is solid and chained to his heart
No key exists that could unlock it. I belong
To him alone. My sufferings are in the soul
I won't allow them to last long

The rainfalls. The rainfalls again on my wounded heart.
I think that my silence and lack of movement is killing my soul
That window in my soul that leads to love
Free me
Free me and give me the luxury to speak what I
Feel in the moment
I have not yet seen the power in containment
The beauty of self-control. There is no point in waiting.

IN THE AFTERMATH

I apologize. I apologize for the part I played
Things shouldn't have been so hard there should never have been such decay
You and I together in this
Should've been beautiful
Musical
I think you misunderstood. I know I misunderstood
And it got kind of hood
I apologize for any disrespect
And I really hate it, if I caused you any regrets
But we are in the journey of life, and sometimes it be's like dat
I know that you forgive me. You know that I forgive you
And we can move on because both of our hearts are true
Leave it in the past
Let's just leave it in the past
And love each other in the AFTERMATH
Even in our collision. Even in the tension. Even when I felt I was the victim
You were still beautiful to me, I would've given you almost anything
Almost anything
From the very first moment, you were wanted
So Fluid, So Stunning, So Broken
You are wanted, still wanted
In the AFTERMATH
We can leave it in the past
Let's just leave it in the past
And love each other in the AFTERMATH

HE MADE ME THINK OF YOU

Today I saw a man that made me think of you
His aura, his eyes
Reminded me of a time and place in my life
That time not so long ago, when you consumed me
Your presence dominated me
There was not a day when I
Did not need to see your face, imagine your touch, or hear your voice

In an instant everything that we were came
Back to me
And I felt that yearning again
That desire to hold you
To kiss you just once

I thought that I had moved on
I thought that I had freed my heart
When I freed you
But now I see that I only buried it

I have only given in to the unnatural course of things
Pretending not to need you in this cold, cold world
In this cold, cold world I crave your warmth

But the heat from your embrace would leave me changed
And I would become the woman
That I do not want to be
A woman given over to seduction
And I am done being seduced

By now I know exactly what you do to me
And when I replay the scenes
I remember why I had to leave

We live in two different worlds
To become one with you would be my demise

It would be the day that darkness
Would begin to shine
The loss of my own beauty would be too much
To bare
I know that I am rare

To deny myself
To break your hold over my soul
I go on

Seeing the world differently
Cherishing the difference in me

It's funny that I saw a man that made me think of you

COLLIDE

It's funny how worlds collide
And how I find myself here for a second time
In the place outside of reality and way too
Close to fantasy
It's crazy how worlds collide
And how tricks play on my mind
I don't feel like I can really see everything going on
Inside of me
I feel my heart starting to crave
And I know that will never do
I see my soul starting to crave
I need to be walking in truth
I shall detach myself
And get help, quickly, swiftly
Before the charade begins again
I will stop and seek out the heart
Of my king or I will shift
Become dumb and dense
I won't play games at all
I will not manipulate situations
I will speak the truth and see
Where things fall
It's funny how worlds collide
And how death comes before life
Let your truth reign
Let me be in your reality
Destiny calls

NO

I will not be simple
I will not be ordinary
I will not do as they do
I will not go where they go
I will not say what they say
And
In a world of yes
I say no
The Son has risen on my eyes
I have decided
Ordinary doesn't suit me
Average?
No

DRINKS ON YOU

I see everything so clearly
For so long I have been living in a
Gold-plated haze
Going around in deceptive cycles
Thinking that it was change
New time
New place
Same symptoms
New man
It took me a while
But now I finally understand
You are pretty much the same
And I thought that you were a different kind
But you are impressed by average
And you do just enough to get by
It didn't start off that way
But I guess it never does
Eventually you hurt the ones you love
I like that I am rare, and you like that I am rare
But only behind closed doors
You almost had me thinking that you were the
Exceptional type
That you were a man that craved goodness
A man who lives in the light
But all the signs are there
And I can no longer deny
That I've been fighting for you with my
Eyes closed
I didn't want to watch you become
What I despise
But I find that in your presence I am
Less than myself
You got me thinking crazy, as if beauty resides

Some place else
At the club
On the dance floor
In the vodka and AMFs
With the White girls or the Persian girls
Who don't really care
I could be a freak
I could dumb myself down
I could live like they live
But I'm too smart and too proud
Don't worry about harming me
The damage has been done
I'm not decadent enough
I'm not what you want

I can't love you like I used to love you
Because you're not who you used to be
And if I don't accept the truth, who knows what this friendship will be?
So goodbye
My love
Too much of you has gone down
Drinks on you for everyone
I just won't be around.

HOW DOES SHE LOVE?

I thought that I loved you
But. You did not see me
And because the sun didn't shine upon your heart
When you read my thoughts
You had no clear portrait
Of the rare beauty that stood before you
Full of grace

It is a shame
We would have been timeless together
We should have been timeless together
But you made a rather odd choice for love

I am not angry, only curious at how you would not take my
Expression, but submitted to hers

Tell me, how does she love?

Is it all that you ever dreamed?
Or is it the compromise of what only your soul desires?
Is it a revelation of the stoic reality that you can't have absolutely
Everything that you have waited for?

Tell me, how does she love?

Please say that she is the image of Eve
That she is so magnificent, you are hypnotized at the sight of her
Say that her beauty is the ugliest thing about her
And that her spirit outshines mine

Please say that she has the power to strengthen your will
Say that she pays homage to your greatness and your weaknesses
And that when she speaks, the tone of her voice soothes you and makes
you feel
At peace

Tell me, how does she love?

I am not angry, only curious at how you would not take my
Expression, but submitted to hers
It's just that you made a rather odd choice for love

FREE

It seems like everything is out to entrap me
But I will not be confined
If it is between you or I
I will do whatever it takes to be me
To know my identity
I see in color
I live in beauty
Weightless
Intrigued and Inspired by possibility
I am twirling on top of the universe
Fearless and free
Everything around me glitters and shines
There is no darkness within the divine
I see the world in glow
I awake with the ability to be fluid
Each new day is radiant and translucent
I have a sparkle. There is a twinkle in my eye because
I understand what it means to be alive
Laughter, Hugs, Kisses, and Smiles
Strawberry Ice Cream
The carefree simple things
Why be shy. Why be afraid. Why accept hindrance?
There is no need to be timid when Life is wonderful. Life is
Limitless
I won't be slowed down, I will never back down
I dominate. I delegate. I create.
The stars glimmer, my being shines
Every element aligns
I am Intelligent
I am Brilliant

I see in color
I live in beauty
Weightless
Intrigued and Inspired by possibility
I am twirling on top of the universe
Fearless and free

NEEDING YOU

At this very moment
I feel the urgency of my
Need for You
All the familiar things are becoming
Foreign and at this very instant I know
That the only one I can save is
Myself
I feel the urgency for more of you
You satisfy me totally and completely
The knowledge of your love for me
Creates an impenetrable security
What am I to do with those who
Have chosen to live outside your embrace?
Although they have known your embrace
I feel the urgency of needing you

BREAK AWAY

The time has come for the greatness inside of
Me to emerge
I have become something unfamiliar
And degenerate, because of rebellion
I have refused to live in love
Love changes things
Your love has changed me
It makes me want to be the best version of myself
It makes me want to become new
I am finally seeing the freedom that
Comes in loving you
Now I understand that you alone
Can love me into perfection
But Lord, I pray Your protection
Over my soul, that You would help
Me to be still and let You transform
See, I have this feeling that everything
Starts and ends with me
That in this place of daily surrender
I will arrive at my long-awaited destiny
I have a knowing that how I decide to live
Right now will either unveil a life more beautiful than I've ever dreamed
Or it will lead me into the dungeon where the ordinary are chained?
I say
It will not be so
I cry and shout it out, until I can speak no more
It will not be so
I have done it before
With much less at stake
I have decided again today
I have decided to
BREAK AWAY
BREAK AWAY
BREAK AWAY

LOVE

The word love is tossed around so carelessly in our society. What most people see as love is really an intense like, lust, or infatuation. It is not love. Love will die for you. Love is selfless. Love creates boundaries and Love has no boundaries at all. Love produces trust and forgives. Love is not just longing and deep emotion. Love is raw, eternal, and spiritual all at the same time.

The following poetry is a compilation of thoughts in regards to love. I can't say that my words were always inspired by love. I can say that I was in deep, deep feeling when writing each work. I've come to the conclusion that true love is very deep and spiritual. It goes far beyond emotion and intellect. It is a choice. True love shapes your entire existence and gives you power. We all need to learn of love. When we understand it, then we can give it. When we can live in love and by love, the way that we live our lives will completely change.

HEAVEN KISSED THE EARTH

Heaven kissed the earth
When GOD created you
In His mastery and brilliance
He gave the gift of you

The perfection of beauty
With so many flaws
The dead man walking
With so many walls

Heaven kissed the earth
Long and sweet
With no sense of time
Without being discreet

Sealing the things that I already knew
The Greatness of GOD
How He is glorious and true
Just to look in your eyes, to see your smile
To be in your presence. I know
GOD is Excellent

You are divine

Despite your chaotic mind

You are priceless and very costly

You are adored even in rejection

You are loved, although bitterness
Has been your companion

Heaven kissed the earth with frantic passion
Taking the longest to part ways
Stepping out of eternity into time
Leaving the splendor of you behind

How could anyone say that there is no GOD?
And that His love isn't great for us all
It is crystal and so transparent
His love is unconditional and strong

I know GOD loves
For He gave the pleasure of you
I know GOD loves
For He placed such treasure in you

Some of them are buried and hidden
Others are daily on display
Your movement and execution
Your giving heart, the dimples on your handsome face

So I have lived to behold greatness
Crafted by the Master Potter's hand
And my love for Him grows deeper
I am amazed by His purpose and plan

You must never forget and never cease to see
You are fearfully and wonderfully made
You have a destiny

Heaven kissed the earth
When GOD created you
In His mastery and brilliance
He gave the gift of you

THE PERFECT DAY

I wish you were here with me right now
It is the perfect day for you and me
It is the perfect day
To take our fill of ecstasy
You should be here
With me right now
Seconds seem to drag
Because you are not near
And I don't think that I can bear it
I must look into your eyes
I need to touch you
Where are you, My Love?
I am pacing
I cannot stand still
I must be going crazy
I swear that I just heard your voice
Are you calling for me?
I should be kissing you right now
Why do you make me wait?
Please come to me
Don't make me beg, My Love.
You know that I will
I will do everything or nothing at all
Just tell me what you want
Your wish is my command
But you must come to me first
With every moment that you are away
I am growing hungry
You will be awhile
But I am ready for you right now
It is the perfect day for you and me

LOVING YOU IS

Loving you is painful
Every moment that you do not touch me
Kills me
Every single moment
Loving you is chaotic
I feel as if I have no control
Everything stops when you walk into the room
And I am surprised to see that my heart is still beating
I have no restraint
All discipline vanishes when I look into your eyes
I can't even think
I lose my train of thought when you are close to me
And instead of being free
Loving you binds me up
It is the entrapment of my very soul
You are too beautiful
You are too much

YOU TRAP ME IN TIME

You trap me in time
Everyday becomes suspended
And at a glance, at a fleeting
Thought of you, all other things become frivolous
You trap me in time
And tomorrow ceases to exist
Sanity flees me and I undermine
Consequence

ENTRANCED

I promise that I am not crazy
I know that you must think that I am insane
How I so openly kiss the ground you walk on
How I bow before you as if you were a god.
You are
The closest thing to divinity
Why else would I love you with my life?
I promise that I am not delusional
I know that you must think that I have gone mad
How I live just to hear you speak
How you are my consistent place of worship
I pay homage to your body
Every single time that I touch you
And even when we are not touching at all
I sit and stare
Idolizing every contour of your face
I promise that I'm not psychotic
I am just entranced

MY WILL

Please put your hand against my
Chest
Can't you hear the sound of my heart
Beating
Glance quickly into my eyes
You don't even have to hold our stare
All I need is a few seconds
Everything that I am thinking will come to you

If you would take a moment to observe
The tilt of my head, the slant in my body
And the curve of my lips
You will notice
How I want you near me

Be a gentleman and open your hand
I shall place my will there
Do what you will
Manipulate it
Break it
Mold it
Bend it

I don't care
Only take care, and
Control it
My will
I will
For you

UNDONE

I look into your eyes and I see
Beauty undiscovered.
Everything about you speaks of
Something greater
So I want to go beyond the surface and learn
Who you really are
I look into your eyes and I am drawn into an
Ocean of mystery knowing that what lies beneath
The serene waters is a strong current capable of destroying
Anything in its path
But when I touch your hand I feel tenderness there, and the need to be
loved in a more selfless way
When I hear you speak I see your heart
And I become undone
I want to soothe you
I want to use you
I want to learn you

MY LOST LOVE

My Lost Love,
I'm trying. I don't want to be
Cold
But you have taken my heart
My heart was so soft, so warm, and so fertile
But in your hand it is swiftly freezing over
And I
I'm so sensitive, so sweet
I'm beginning to lose all feeling
You are making me numb and bitter
The eyes that once held compassion have evolved
Along with compassion, they hold deceit and manipulation
The lips that I once beckoned to my own have leaked out venom
In the form of unworthy lovers
And so I know that there is poison in your kiss
But I would say kiss me still
And it makes me ill. I am sickened by my own lack of reason
And, Lost Love,
What about your hands?
The ones that possess such strength and tenderness
The hands that I would rather caress me
They are now choking the life out of me
And I can hardly breathe,
Lost Love,
Why have you denied me your embrace?
Why have you not called out for me?
Or even searched for me?
Why have you not given me your smile?
Or words of passion and desire?
Do you not know? Don't you know?
I would be seduced by you. I would sleep

Peacefully in your arms
My heart storms, it rages inside
Yet my soul is in need of you
And my body often screams for you
And I am ashamed of these truths
But Lost Love,
What am I to do?
It is better to become hard so that I will not be moved by your
Unspoken rejection
It is better to become blind, so that I cannot see the passion that isn't
for me
It is better to become deaf, so that I don't hear your soothing voice and
arousing words
Love,
I am lost
I am drifting away
Every single day. I am drifting away
I am lost for words
I am lost for your love
I am beginning to be appalled by your touch
Soon I will no longer desire you
I always knew that you were a fool
My Lost Love,
How shall I go on when you act this way?
Maybe you don't see me
But how can that be?
When I carry my heart in my eyes
Would you free me, and tell me truthfully,
Truthfully,
Have I lost?
Have I lost in loving you, wanting you,
My Lost Love?

THE PUNISHMENT

You've given me no room to step beyond the boarder
Although you have crossed the line once or twice before
I went outside of the calm into turbulent waters, even when you told me
not to go
I took the risk anyway and almost drowned us all beneath the waves
When I made it to shore you were already there, but you stood at a
distance watching me
Cough and gasp for air. I was fighting for my life, you didn't make a sound
You just turned emotionally violent and cold, just like the other one
But you have been near death, and you have actually died
Shots were fired at you more than once
They have come for you multiple times
I never left your side
You even held the loaded gun
And pulled the trigger on yourself
Your blood splattered on me
Those were the times of uncertainty
In adversity I would never let you endure it alone
I never even changed my tone
I felt the knives in my back and the dagger in my heart
I didn't make a sound, I barely said a word
Because I know who you are and I understand we are all flawed
So, I stayed with you in the trenches, I fought in a battle that wasn't even
mine
I believe in you so powerful, so divine
To cut you off, to leave you, to hold it against you never even crossed my
mind
Maybe that was me being foolish
But now that I've fallen you have refused to catch me
I know that I unintentionally and intentionally
Made you a casualty of war

I apologized for that
But you still sentence me to death
And walk off into the sunset
Holding the hand of another flawed one
A repeat offender
With a criminal background darker than mine
A repeat offender
Who hasn't even put in half of half of the time?
The wise get lost, the saint sins
We become blind
But if you push rewind, you will find that
I have LOVED YOU MORE THAN I HAVE EVER HURT YOU
And your punishment does not fit my crime.

THE LOOK OF YOU

What is this?
What are you doing to me?
And why can't I be free?
Already my thoughts wander
To you
It's nothing said or done
But today it was the look of you
How you sat carelessly in your chair
How beautifully wild and electric
Unshaven and clean-cut
I am longing to feel your touch
Even the simplicity of your attire
Struck a certain wire
And I felt so drawn
I wonder if you feel me
When I am near you
It is a struggle
I think on things that I should not
Then you smile so seductively
Or is it just me?
Am I imagining things?
You just undo me
Too quickly my thoughts wander to you
Today it was just the look of you

STOP MY HEART

Sometimes I wish that I COULD JUST STOP MY HEART.
My heart seems to have a mind of its own
I have no idea how to satisfy its appetite for love.
I try to harness my soul
And I tell my heart not to move so fast, but it just ignores me
And in an instant my heart has given itself away
My heart doesn't even ask me
And then I am left for dead

What shall I do?
Now that I know that I am in love with you?
What shall I say when you have taken my breath away?
Where can I go
If it is not where you are?
How would I live
If I can't be with you?

I have been waiting for so long
And finally you have come
Now my soul can be free
You are what I want
My choice
My destiny
I honestly don't know what to do
Now that I know, I love you

Is there anyone who can tell me
If it is natural for you to be my everything
Am I dysfunctional for basking and soaking in your love

Everything is moving and I cannot stop

I'm not sure
What to do

Now that I know, I love you.

WILD FOR YOU

I am drained
Worn out, from
Wanting you so badly
My heart is tired, from
Beating so steadily and wild
For you
My eyelids are heavy and my sight
Is dim from such optimistic vision
Looking, seeing into who you really are
And blinded by who you could be
My legs
They are unstable and limp from
Standing for you so long
And my soul is drenched with mud
From the
Journey of loving you
With all
And so strongly
My ears can't hear a thing
Because you only whisper
And your words are so faint
That they drift away with the
Wind
And my mind . . . My psychological mind
My mind plays tricks on me
When it comes to you
Oh, how I often look for clues
I don't know a thing. I wonder about
Everything
I am drained, worn, from wanting
Sleepless from wanting
But
My heart beats on
Wild for You

GOD

The following selection is the most intimate written in this book. The poetry is vivid and transparent. They are more emotional than spiritual. These are conversations with God about how I was feeling at the time and not the truth of the situation. I believe that being humble and transparent before God is so vital in processing life, but that is a private intimate place between you and God. When nobody else understands, He does. When everyone else may judge you because of your flaws, or weakness, He won't. I have found unconditional love and acceptance in the presence of God. There is nothing that I can't say to Him.

His love passes natural understanding. He is able to handle my feelings. His love breathes hope and faith into my soul. You can process things from a spiritual place or an emotional place. These writings are very emotional and in the moment. So, in these poems I say the things that I "should not say" to my God. Then I am still, and I just exhale, and I let God love me. I let Him love me out of despair, confusion, frustration, and self-condemnation.

There is such a power and strength that comes from being loved by God. His love gives me the will to live. The love of Christ is perfection. His love can transform your life. The strength of His love will still the wild storm of emotion that threatens to destroy you. That is what this entire poetry book is about. He doesn't want anything but relationship. Relationship with God is the key to living a peaceful and productive life. Give in to the love of Christ. You won't regret it.

LOVE ME BACK TO LIFE

Things have never been so dark before
All of my strength is gone
I have nothing left to give
Something has stolen my song
I can't hear the sweet melodies
And all my rhythm has faded
Even the beat of my heart is faint
I don't think that I am going to make it

I would smile
Feel serenity if death came to me
I would leave this life and feel
Tranquility
It seems death has come for me

You know my heart
I want to live
I love to watch sunrises
But I cannot move
I can't sit up
I can't even open my eyes

But if
You love me right now
Before I die

Will You Love Me Back to Life?

Love me back to life
Love me back to life
Or else I will not survive

Please forgive my frailty
But
You are my only clarity

I know that I've been cold and numb
But Your touch is all that I need
To feel, to have warmth

Will you Love Me Back to Life?
Breathe strength into my hallow soul
Take Your lips and kiss me
Leave Your imprint
Give me hope

The despair has planted itself in me
And there is no freedom as far as my eyes can see
I know that you are so much greater than me
I know that you are everything I need

If
You have a plan for me

Will you Love Me Back to Life?

Love Me Back to life
Love Me Back to life
Right Now
Tonight
Or else I will not survive

FROM THE DEAD

When did I die?
When did I become so lifeless and destitute?
When did I become one with the normal and foolish?
When did I lose my pride and self-worth?
How did I suffer memory loss? And completely forget my lineage?
I am so tired of it all
I remember clearly
There was no exact moment, just a very slow descent
Inch by inch, and over time
You faded from my dreams. How could I let You fade away?
You were all that I dreamed of
You gave every single thing meaning
You were my reason
But then my thoughts drifted from You
I was no longer consumed
And every day the dirt was shoveled up
And my grave was dug
I was no longer taken by You
And with every day that I lived outside Your embrace
The dirt was thrown on me
Now I am buried alive
Crying out for peace
Begging for deliverance
Seeking salvation
From a cruel and cold world
Darkness surrounds me
My speech is slurred
My head is down
I used to always be looking up
Standing in response to your unforgettable
Touch.

My Lord,
Revive me
Breathe new life into me
Raise me from the dead
Let me live again
Forgive my adultery
Take me again; bring me back from the dead

CPR

GOD, HELP ME
GOD, TOUCH ME
I am numb
My habits, my addictions
These rituals have overtaken me
And I have gone away
I think that I am lost
Although most of my thoughts are on You
I often think about how You have already
Freed me and I am paralyzed
Confounded by my own stupidity
The truth haunts me on a daily
Basis and still I remain old
I feel tired and torn
With each new sunrise I convince myself that
I should go on and live
But I hate what I have become
I am robotic
I am irreverent
I am prideful and rebellious
And I don't even know when I became this way
Dignity has left me
As I stagger to maintain my appearance
My inner beauty flees
Then eventually I am left with me
I want to vomit
I cry. I don't sleep at night
Because I know how I hurt You
I just sit.
Thinking on the things I should do, and how I
Really ought to be
But what I have become is awful
I am a monster
And Father,

I want my beauty back
What would it take for us to kiss again?
What must I do to rendezvous with You?
I am willing to do anything
But I feel that I am unable
I must shine again
GOD, HELP ME
GOD, TOUCH ME
Have mercy and
Resuscitate
My heart, my soul
I need to be reborn
Everything about me must become new
Wash me, baptize me, and drown me in
Your all-consuming love
And I know that I would want to live again
I am sure that I would come to my senses
And try to live again
Otherwise, I will go insane
Tonight I will rest in
Your love and
Because my heart is open
Because
My Spirit begs for Your touch
Your angels will minister to me
I will awaken light
With every burden removed.
I have lifted up my dark soul to You once again
Because I know
You
Are faithful and true
I know that You love me
More
More than I could ever love myself
I fall asleep with hope
And I rise with peace

FAR AWAY FROM YOU

All that I am seems far away from You
Everything except the deepest place of my heart
My whole being rests in You
And without Your love, I have absolutely no reason
My Lord, My God. My Friend.
The entire world beckons me
Daily they ask, they seek my devotion
And lately my strength is fading and my will is shaking
My heart screams for You
I have almost lost my voice
I can see it in my choices
I can hear it in my tone
I know it by my thoughts
And how I meditate
Emotions run from the stable place
All that I am seems Far Away From You
And I need to see
I must see Your face
I want You, and nothing else
I will for You and You alone
In the weakest moments
My actions don't show it
But the deepest places, the corridors
Of my Spirit, Soul, and Body
I Will
ALWAYS
Be in need of You
You are my Father and I accept truth
Pour out Your mercy once again
Grace me; let Your beauty sing to me
Let Your glory radiate me

Let Your wisdom enlighten me
Everything becomes clear
When I am at Your side
You are the love of my life
And I will reach for You
I will search for You
And as I find You
Peace comes. My Lord. Thank You for Eternal Peace.

I HAVE BEEN HERE

I have been here
I've had this conversation
With myself before
God, save me from myself
God, show me truth
Let me live Your way. Do it Your way
I am at a loss. I don't know what to do
I'm not sure how to be
I am growing weary of routine
And solitude
Is it time?
May I step out of time, Lord?
I will not have an evil heart of unbelief
I will be satisfied by You
I am satisfied in Your love, Your hold, Your embrace
But Lord, show me today. Show me now
How much You are in love with me
Bless me. Kiss me. Breathe on me and in me
Show me my place of freedom
How do I step out of time in this?
Turn turmoil into a masterpiece
Lord,
Show me
Your way
I give in to
You
I told You long ago that I wanted You first, that I wanted to be like You
I asked for grace.
For You to make me into the woman You created me to be
Show me the adjustments. How do I love you more?
Let me see your movement
In me and around me

UNLOCKED

Thank You for unlocking my soul
For putting up with all my wrong
For giving me room to breathe
For making my dirty heart clean
Thank You for seeing past my consistent crimes
For maintaining Your deity in the midst
Of my ridiculous pride
I have been unlocked
Released from deceit
Freed from obscene mentalities
Renewed to kingdom realities
Brought out of the place that I used to be
Into the place I was meant to be
I must be with You, Savior
I must be in You, Redeemer
I am nothing without You.

WHAT CAN I GIVE?

What can I give to You?
How can I show You
The depth of my heart,
The intensity of my quest?
Lord, I must know You
I won't accept anything less

There is a place in me
That craves Your presence
I must be with You
Or
I will not go on

It storms all around me
Everything thunders
The rain screams
Violent realities
Society pursues me
They say I should be like them

But the most intimate parts of my heart speak
Cautioning me
Of the eternal hunger that would be
If I were to ever let go of such a perfect love

My entire being is in You, My Lord
The beauty of Your blessing sustains me
I am in constant overflow
Consistently overwhelmed
By how majestic and powerful
You are

I search You
My eyes seek Your Glory
And with every moment
I am changed by what I see

You hold undiscovered treasures in Your hand
The unknown places of God
The untold secrets in God
That is my destination

I will walk with You until my legs have no more strength
Even then I will crawl to be near Your tenderness
I would be Your shadow
I will to reflect Your image
I will be beautiful just like You

And while the world blindly searches for meaning
In the cold arms of man-made philosophy
Atonement has come for me
Your love pursues me

And I rest
As I seek
To find that places in You
That are yet to be found

IN YOU

Father,
I need You in my life
Everything around me rages
And so, at times I am in a rage
I am stupid and dumb
An educated fool, without You
Father,
If there was ever a day that I needed to see You
Face-to-face
It is today
Right now
In this moment
Because more often than not
It has been a struggle
But I find my rest in You
You are my strength
My ability
My sufficiency
I need to live in You
I was made to be with You
My peace is found in You.

EMOTIONS RAGE

So many emotions rage
Calm only comes when I think on You
As I meditate on Your goodness and faithfulness
Peace rises up inside my soul
As I look into Your eyes
Every uncertainty disappears
I am at rest
I no longer ponder
On the exploits of man
What others are doing is made irrelevant
All expectations of man die
My security and success stand in the promise
Of Your word
It is in the secret place that calm comes
The worries that try to bombard me
Hold no power
I simply step out of the way
And lay them at Your feet
There is nothing to fear at all
I do not fear at all
You have made a way for me
Your mercy has paved a path
Directly into Your will
As I am still
As I bow down
As I pray
As I obey
Calm comes
Rest comes
Peace resides
Because
I know
My God

SPEAK TO ME

I stand in this place
In Your beautiful presence
With nothing left to say
Every word falls to the ground
Your piercing love has captured me
For far too long we've been in love
And most times, I've been consumed with me

The moment has come for me to listen
I will be silent; I will not speak
Finally, I'm in position
I must clearly hear Your voice
Speak to me
I am undone, My King, My Lord
Speak to me, speak to me
Your power speaks to me

Your perfect love will lead me
You've freed me
One word is all I need.

ONLY YOU

Only You can look deep down
Inside me, and know
Everything that I deny
Shine the light on the
Hidden parts of me
And help me face all the things I despise
It seems that there is wickedness
That has latched onto my soul
And I know by my
Very own thoughts and responses
That desire has gained control
Something has taken root
And now clings to my thoughts
I remember putting it to death
But maybe not
I thought it was dead
Yet I find it resurfaces in my heart
It seems that my appetite
Is still supreme
I am unsettled by my need
How I allow my mind to ponder on lower things
I must judge my intentions
And be honest about what they are
It is a sad reality,
The desire in my heart
How could I be so silly?
To indulge in this constant longing
How can I be so shattered?
From the inside out
When I already know the truth
The way he acts out

No integrity
No empathy
Doing things
Secretly
To satisfy his own needs
Although it would hurt me
Why have these emotions
Birthed in me?
Why do I feel he can satisfy me?
Even when he takes life from me
How dumb can I be?
But in reality
I am strong
I know what is going on
My intention
Is to do the wrong things
To feed this deadly craving
Have mercy
It is up to me to choose life
To live in peace
It is not up to you
I know it is up to me

NOT WITHOUT YOU

Everything fails me
And at times I fight to keep the skeletons back
To erase that time and place that had me lost
In so many ways
The darkest parts in me
Lurking, hypnotizing me
Exposing the fool in me
At times the shame hangs like a condemned man's chains
Keeping my sanity confined
Purposefully embracing grime, pleading the fifth, acting blind
Saying that I would deny myself the next time
But in each act I grow cold
Growing more bold in my hunger, more careless
And greedy in the ways that I indulge
The place of repentance is harder and harder to find
The desire is so strong
And my lifestyle is compromised
I used to be wise
I used to cry
Now my soul is numb, I am dry
And the truth is that I've become a dumb one
And still You call out for my love
Even when I have broken Your heart
I have been ruthless, and still You call out for me, to me
Blessing me with the kiss of life
Healing waters of forgiveness flow
And I am cleansed
Your word purifies me
And my faith is made whole again
Lord, I love You.
My life is nothing without You
I am lost without You
But I am not without You

STANDING THERE

I fall on my knees
Because I need you so much
I need you to be who I am
I need you to be who you've said I am
The sun has been bright
The rain has fallen
The skies have thundered
My soul has been wounded by the lightning
The dust has settled
And when all the smoke has cleared
I see you
Standing there
Apart from the crowd
Far away from the noise
And you beckon me into a still and quiet place
I look into your eyes and I know that I should be with you
I should be with you and only you
You and only you
How can it be that my entire being longs for you?
How is it that all I desire is to make you smile
How is it that I lag and slow around before entering into your embrace
When all I really want
Is to be with you and only you
I see you
Standing there
Apart from the crowd
Far away from the noise
And you beckon me into a still and quite place
I fall on my knees
Because I need you
I need you
To be
Who I really am

SHIELD

I knew that You would keep me
I knew that You would protect me
From the shame
Thank you, My Father, for Your
Never-ending mercy
Oh, how I need Your grace
In every moment
In every instance
Your goodness was a shield for me
And I will spend my lifetime declaring
The testimony of Your never-ending love

FATHER

My Father
Have mercy
Forgive me for all this insanity
Forgive me for embracing this
Calamity.
My soul is drained`
I am so tired of it all
I feel too much
I give too much
And to some, what I am
Isn't good enough
My Lord, please dry my tears, please
Erase all of my fears and
Take me in Your arms once again
This pain is only for a moment
I need You for a lifetime
I love You
I love You so much
But lately You haven't been consuming my thoughts
All I know is that I am better than this
So much better than this
Heal my distraught soul
Open my blinded eyes and remove the wax from my deaf ears
See your servant
See this heart of mine
Know that all that I am is made for You
I am so lost and insignificant without Your love
I must have Your touch
I must have Your presence in my life
My Lord
You are life

My God
Lift me up
Bring me into the place that I belong
I am hungry for Your exact will
I will stay with You
In You, Lord
Strip me bare
And rebuild me
Have mercy
Surely
Your goodness
And
Your mercy shall follow me
All the days of my life

FINALLY

Finally. I fade away
Totally into You
Everyday my spirit speaks
Beckoning me to be more
Like Your shining light
I've walked out of a deep, dark pit
Into eternal bliss, and limitless peace
Everything finally fades away
And my being displays
The truth of Your love
The healing in Your touch
I have made the exchange
Finally I fade away
And stand up straight
In Your boundless love
I thank You, Lord, for Your Glory
I thank You for how much You adore me
Finally
I fade away
Totally into You

Printed in the United States
By Bookmasters